ICE!

POEMS ABOUT POLAR LIFE

DOUGLAS FLORIAN

HOLIDAY HOUSE · NEW YORK

CONTENTS

THE POLAR REGIONS

Two polar regions on our Earth,
and not a third or fourth.
Antarctica is farthest south,
the Arctic farthest north.
The ends of Earth,
the most remote,
so far from the equator,
each pole's a frosty, frozen place,
an Earth refrigerator.

THE POLAR REGIONS, also known as the frigid zones, are found at the two pole ends of Earth. The Arctic is at the very north of the globe and the Antarctic is at the very south. Life in these habitats is difficult, with extremely cold temperatures and strong winds. The polar regions get less of the sun's heat and light energy because the sun's radiation comes at an angle rather than in a direct line. Also the snow and ice reflect much of the sunlight, adding to the cold. Due to the tilt of Earth's axis, both regions get twenty-four hours of daylight in summer and total darkness at mid-winter.

ANTARCTICA

Antarctica's a continent—
more south you cannot go.
The coldest, driest place on Earth,
and mostly ice and snow.
It's frigid and it's freezing
and a wicked wind there blows.
The penguins there look SO well-dressed,
although they don't wear clothes.
Antarctica's a glacial land.
It's never warm there, is it?
It's not a place I'd like to live
but an ICE place to visit!

ANTARCTICA is a continent, part of the Earth's crust. It is mostly covered by a huge sheet of ice up to 2.5 miles thick. The temperatures may average -76 degrees Fahrenheit. Few animals can survive the cold winter there, but during the summer many animals such as penguins, whales, seals, and seabirds visit Antarctica to enjoy its rich food supply. The Southern Ocean is home to a variety of plant and animal life, including starfish, sea anemones, coral, and sponges (some of which may live hundreds of years). Ten species of whales live in the Southern Ocean. They travel to warmer waters during the Antarctic winter. Moss and lichens live on the rocky landscapes of Antarctica.

EMPEROR PENGUIN

I am the emperor.
The emperor of ice.
Three below zero
is my paradise.
I am the emperor.
I am the king.
All of Antarctica's
under my wing.
I am the emperor.
I'm regal and royal.
Here it's so freezing that
nothing can spoil.
I am the emperor.
I am the lord.

My pointed long beak
catches fish like a sword.
I am the emperor.
An imperial bird.
I hatch from an egg,
and I'm feathered not furred.
I am the emperor.
I rule from on high.
I'm mighty almighty—
too bad I can't fly!

EMPEROR PENGUINS are the largest penguins on Earth. They can grow to be four feet tall and weigh up to one hundred pounds. With their streamlined bodies and flipper-like wings, they are well suited for swimming. Penguins can dive hundreds of feet deep in the cold ocean waters near Antarctica. There they feed on fish, squid, and krill. They nest on the ice during winter. After the female lays a large egg, she transfers it to the male, who keeps it warm atop his feet with his brood pouch, a warm fold of skin on his abdomen. After two months, the egg hatches and the female returns to care for the chick as the male goes off to feed.

THE ARCTIC

The Arctic is
quite stark a place—
the northernmost on Earth.
The ice is slowly melting there,
diminishing in girth.
The Arctic's home to lots of life,
both animals and plants.
But **we** must slow down climate change—
it may be **their** last chance.

THE ARCTIC region is at the northernmost end of planet Earth. The center of the Arctic Circle is mostly frozen ice floating on the Arctic Ocean, but the edges include parts of Canada, Greenland, Iceland, Russia, Finland, Denmark, Norway, Sweden, and the United States. Animals that live in the Arctic include the polar bear, the Arctic hare, the gray wolf, and the Arctic fox. Because of global warming, the Arctic ice is shrinking, threatening the habitat of life there. Land masses in the Arctic region are mainly tundra. Here the land is flat, and only hardy low-lying plants such as mosses, grasses, and lichens can grow in the very cold and windy weather. Arctic areas have been inhabited by people for thousands of years. These include the Inuit people of Greenland, Alaska, and Canada.

THE TUNDRA

Frozen ground.
Hardly a sound.
Lacking trees.
Minus degrees.
Strong winds blow.
Frosty snow.
A harsh, severe place:
Arctic tundra.
Yet there's
life there—
That's the wondra!

The severe winds, frozen ground, and bitter cold weather of THE TUNDRA limit the plants and animals that can survive there. Animals that live in the tundra must adapt to long and very cold winters. Mammals and birds there insulate their bodies with fat. During winter, when food is scarce, many animals migrate south or hibernate. Short plants with shallow roots also adapt to the harsh winds, thin soil, and frozen subsoil called permafrost. Low shrubs, mosses, grasses, and lichens can survive the Arctic tundra, but trees cannot.

POLAR BEAR

She slum-bears when
the year is late
(but doesn't truly
hi-bear-nate).
Her heavy white fur coat is full
to make cold weather bear-able.
Fur on her arms.
Fur on her nose.
Fur on her ears.
Fur on her toes.
Fur on her elbows
and her knees.
That's why she rarely
needs to sneeze!

POLAR BEARS are massive hunters of the Arctic and the largest bears on Earth. Males can weigh close to a ton. Females are much smaller. The diet of polar bears consists mainly of seals, which they catch as the seals emerge at their breathing holes in the ice. Two layers of dense fur and a thick layer of fat keep polar bears warm. Their fur is also waterproof, enabling them to swim in the extremely cold water of the Arctic. Polar bear cubs are born and raised in a cozy den dug in the snow by their mother. Many scientists believe that global warming is a serious danger to the survival of polar bears since the melting of sea ice reduces the habitat where they can hunt seals.

BLUE WHALE

The largest animal ever on Earth.
Wide as an airplane in its girth.
And head to tail it's just as long.
But yet it stops to sing a song.
And though a blue whale cannot fly,
it loves to leap up toward the sky.
The bones in each flipper resemble a hand,
which means that its ancestors lived on land.
The whale's a tale of evolution—
without an airplane's air pollution.

The BLUE WHALE is one of many species of whales that migrate to cold polar seas to feed on krill during summer months. They travel to warmer waters to give birth. Blue whales were hunted almost to extinction by commercial whalers until their harvesting was banned in 1967. Most of them migrate to warmer seas when winter comes. The blue whale is the largest animal to ever live on Earth, larger than any dinosaur. The longest blue whale is as long as an Airbus A319 jet and can weigh up to 200 tons. Its heart alone may weigh 400 pounds! The bones of a whale's flipper resemble a hand, which means that it probably evolved from a creature that once lived on land. Blue whales feed mostly on krill, small shrimp-like crustaceans. They can eat 40 million krill in a day. Blue whales are now rare because they were hunted for their meat and blubber. They are now an endangered species.

KRILL

Fish and penguins, squids and seals,
all find krill make splendid meals.
Blue whales eat krill by the millions:
Millions! Billions! Trillions! Krillions!

KRILL are shrimp-like creatures that grow to a length of about two inches. Krill live in the waters of both the Arctic and Southern seas. Though small in size, they are a big part of the food chain of sea creatures and are eaten by penguins, seals, whales, squid, and fish. A blue whale may eat as many as 40 million krill a day. That's a meal of about four tons! Antarctic krill are perhaps the most abundant species on Earth, as they may number up to 400 trillion.

ARCTIC FOX

The Arctic fox—a crafty guy;
it's cunning, clever, smart, and sly.
Its four fox feet have furry soles
to tunnel into burrow holes.
Its bushy thick fur tail is built
to warm him like a cozy quilt.

The fur of the **ARCTIC FOX** fox in summer is grayish brown in color to help camouflage it against the rocks of the tundra. By the winter, its fur has grown thick and is white to match the snow-covered landscape. The thick bushy tail (called a "brush") of the Arctic fox can be wrapped over its body like a quilt to keep it warm while sleeping. Compared to other foxes, the Artic fox has short legs and small ears. This helps its body to conserve heat. The soles of its feet are furry, and it can burrow into snow with them or go into the abandoned burrow of another animal. The Arctic fox hunts small animals such as voles, lemmings, and birds, but it may also eat berries and insects.

MUSK OX

The fully woolly musk ox bull
is known for his loud bellow.
And if he's large, then he will charge
another musk ox fellow.

The fully woolly musk ox cow
knows how to cross the tundra.
With such a baggy, shaggy coat
it's hard to see what's undra.

Please take my word
a musk ox herd
should be approached most gently.
Don't make much noise (for that annoys)
or push one ox-idently.

The MUSK OX lives mostly in the Canadian Arctic and Greenland. It has two layers of woolly fur and a thick layer of fat to keep warm. A short fur undercoat is covered by a long shaggy outercoat of guard hairs that reach almost to the ground. Both males (bulls) and females (cows) have large curved horns to defend against wolves. When a musk ox herd is threatened, the bulls and cows face outward in a ring to protect the calves. A musk ox uses its keen sense of smell to find food under snow. Its hooves have sharp edges to crack through the crust of snow or ice and eat the grasses, moss, roots, and lichens on the ground.

WALRUS

I'm massive, heavy, weighty, husky.
My whiskers are long.
My teeth are tusky.
I weigh two tons.
I'm hardly small.
Call me wall-rus, for I'm a wall!

The **WALRUS** is a very large marine mammal that normally lives in the Arctic. Males usually weigh between one and two tons, while the females weigh about two thirds as much. Walruses have two tusks, which are actually elongated teeth. The males use their tusks for fighting and dominating other males. Walruses have massive amounts of blubber under their skin. This helps them to keep warm and gives them energy. They have thick wrinkled skin and an air sac under their throats, which helps them float in the water. The four large flippers of a walrus enable it to swim well but are also used to move about on land. Walruses are hunted by polar bears on land and killer whales at sea.

24

ARCTIC HARE

My winter coat is totally white.
My summer coat is gray.
And should it rain,
I can't complain:
I'm having a bad *hare* day.

ARCTIC HARES grow a coat of white fur in winter to blend into their surroundings, but some may have a gray coat in summer to match the rocks of their habitat. To conserve heat, they have shortened ears and legs and lots of body fat compared to hares in warmer climates. They feed upon willow leaves, mosses, berries, roots, and lichens. With their good sense of smell, they can find food buried beneath the ground. Arctic hares are hunted by many animals, such as the gray wolf, Arctic fox, Canada lynx, ermine, and snowy owl. To escape these predators, they may run up to 40 miles per hour for short spurts. These hares are active all year long and do not hibernate.

SEAL

On land they're lumbering, clumsy, and s l o w .
For they lack legs with which to go.
But in the sea their speed is great.
In sea, all seals can seal-ebrate.

The Arctic is home to several species of SEALS, including most typically ringed seals and bearded seals. These so-called *ice seals* all live on or near sea ice. There are six species of Antarctic seals, including leopard seals, Ross seals, and Antarctic fur seals. Seals are very awkward getting about on land, inching along on their bellies and, unlike walruses, not helped at all by their flippers. They may haul onto land to rest, to get warm, or to give birth. In the sea, their streamlined body and four flippers help them speed gracefully. They may stay underwater for fifteen minutes before coming up for air. Seals feed upon krill, fish, squid, shellfish, and even birds.

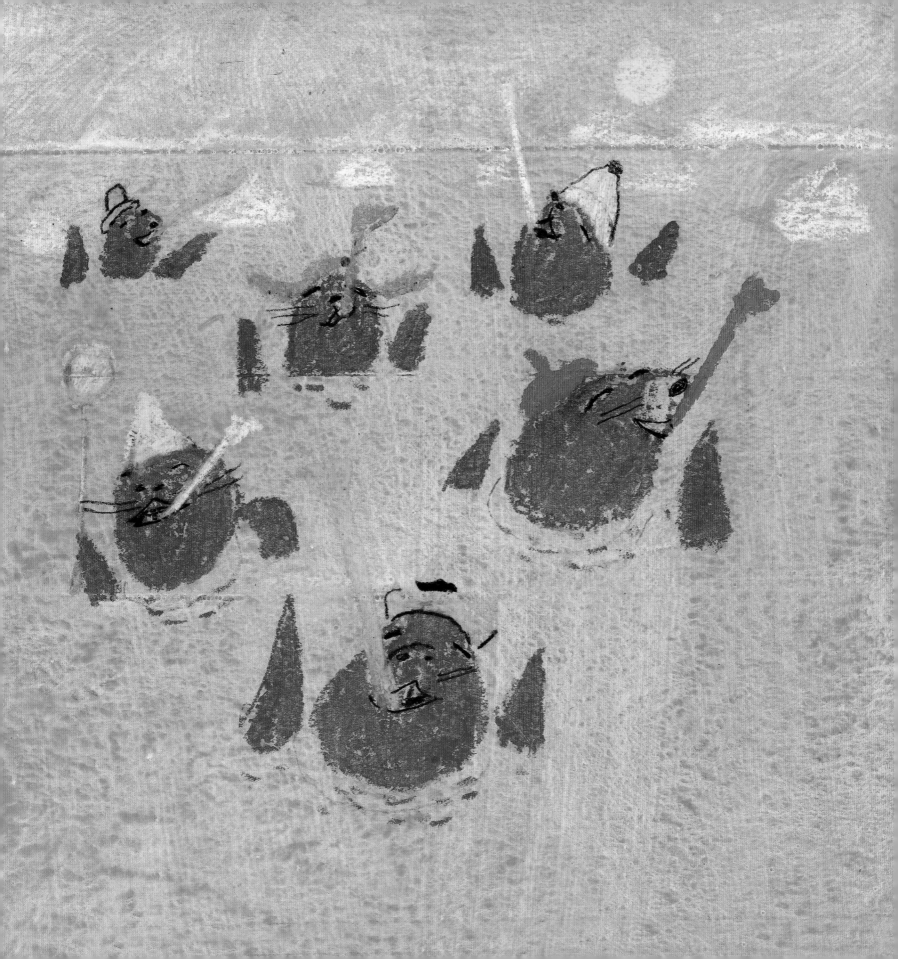

SNOWY OWL

I'm bright.
I'm white.
I'm quite a sight to see.
Make no mistake,
I'm no snowflake.
You'd best be scared of me!

My eyes can spy.
My ears can hear.
All creatures should stay hid.
I quickly catch.
I deftly snatch.
I'm very TALONted.

The **SNOWY OWL** is a large bird of the Arctic tundra. Its ghostly white feathers serve as camouflage against its snow-covered environment. Females have more black flecks or bands on their feathers than males do. The snowy owl's keen eyesight and great hearing help it to hunt. It can even hear prey hiding beneath the snow. This owl's wings have comb-like feather edges called "flutings." These help to muffle any sound as it silently swoops down through the air. With its large, sharp claws (talons), the snowy owl grabs its quarry. Snowy owls feed mostly on lemmings, catching more than a thousand in a year. They may also hunt for rabbits, fish, and birds.

MOOSE

The moose is un-moose-takable,
with mighty height and antlers full.
He has a saggy, baggy nose
and walks along on pointy toes.
He wades in water to his thighs,
escaping gnats, moose-quitos, flies.
A striking sight if you might see him—
like something from an art moose-eum.

The MOOSE is the largest animal in the deer family. A male can weigh almost a ton and stand up to seven and a half feet tall. A moose's hooves are sharp and pointed, so as to get a good grip on ice and snow. Its saggy nose is called a muzzle. During warm weather, a moose may wade in water to avoid flies and other pests. A male moose grows flat-shaped antlers, which are used as weapons to battle rival males. The antlers are shed each year and a new set is grown. The droopy nose of the moose enables it to close its nostrils while feeding on plants under the water.

NARWHAL

Far up **nar**th the **nar**whal goes
among ice-cold scen**ar**ios.
Its **nar**row, spiky spiral spear
provokes extraordi**nar**y fear.
It weighs two tons.
It's long as a car.
The **nar**whal's very
hard to ig**nar**!

The **NARWHAL** is a medium-sized whale that can grow up to eighteen feet long and weigh up to 3,500 pounds. Also known as the "unicorn of the sea," the narwhal travels farther north than any other mammal. In the cold Arctic waters of Canada, Greenland, and Russia, it feeds upon fish such as cod and halibut, and also shrimp and squid. The males grow a long hollow spiral tusk up to ten feet long. It may be used as a sword to battle other males, impress females, or stun a fish. Only about fifteen percent of females also grow a tusk, which is smaller and less spiral.

GRAY WOLF

We hunt together in a pack.
We race and chase and then attack
a beaver, rabbit, deer, or moose.
(Strong jaws and sharp teeth tear flesh loose.)
We whine.
We whoop.
We yelp.
We growwwl.
But most of all
we wolves will
HOWWWWWWWWWL!

GRAY WOLVES are social animals and usually live in packs averaging from five to eleven members. This enables them to hunt more successfully, as they team up against their prey. These wolves cooperate to catch large animals such as musk ox, deer, and moose, but will also eat small mammals, birds, fish, and fruit. Although their eyesight is not strong, they have a keen sense of smell and hearing. They also have agile, strong bodies and long legs to chase their quarry. Wolves communicate with each other through barks, growls, and howls. They may howl to each other to keep in touch with other members of their pack or to warn other packs to keep out of their territory. The winter fur of these wolves is thick and mottled gray in color, although their coats may be white or blackish.

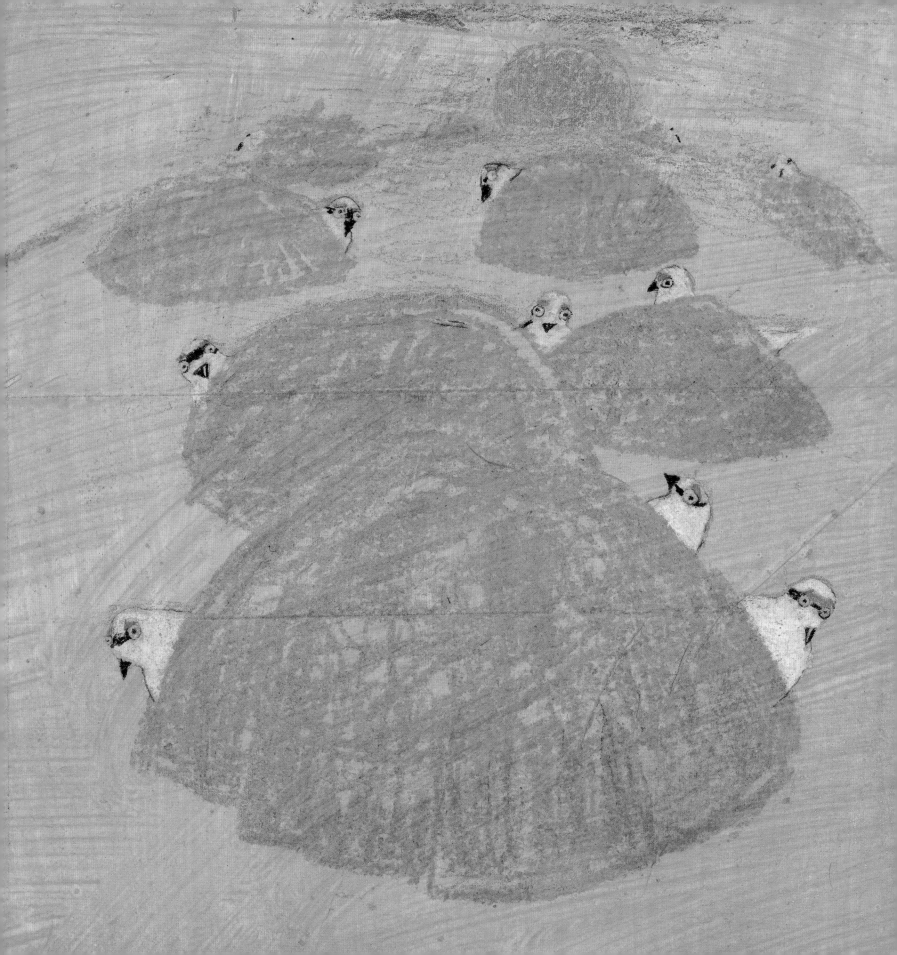

PTARMIGAN
(PRONOUNCED TAR-MA-GIN)

The ptarmagin's a ptimid bird
that ptoddles on the ptundra.
It hides in rocks and crevices—
and ptucks itself in undra.
When ptemperatures are ptemperate,
the ptarmagins are ptan.
Ptill winter comes along and then
they pturn white ptarm-again.

The **PTARMIGAN** of the Arctic is called the rock ptarmigan. It lives in the barren rocky tundra of the countries surrounding the North Pole. The ptarmigan is a well-camouflaged bird year-round. In the winter, its plumage is white except for black tail feathers and dark eyes. The male has large red eyebrows called "combs." In the spring the ptarmigan molts its feathers and grows new ones of mottled brown and gray. It feeds on plant buds, leaves, berries, and flowers. The letter "p" in its name is not pronounced.

WOLVERINE

I am a lean, mean fighting machine,
the fiercest fighter you've ever seen.
I'm muscular and stout and stocky.
Avoid me—you're considered lucky.
I feed with greed.
I love the chase.
They call me a "glutton,"
but **not** to my face!

The WOLVERINE, the largest member of the weasel family, is a muscular, stocky carnivore known for its fighting ferocity. The wolverine is sometimes called a "glutton," perhaps because of its voracious appetite. They often prey upon small mammals such as rabbits, but they can also attack animals as large as caribou. They are primarily found in Arctic and alpine regions of Canada, Alaska, Scandinavia, and Russia. Wolverines can roam 15 miles a day in search of food.

CARIBOU

Look above my head, you'll see
antlers sprouting like a tree—
don't hang your hats or coats on me!
I feed on lichens, leaves, and fruits,
mushrooms, grasses, twigs, and shoots.
I trek across great Arctic routes
upon wide feet—my cariboots.

The **CARIBOU'S** furry wide feet with large hooves act as snowshoes. They distribute the animal's weight, preventing it from sinking into deep snow. The hollowed-out hooves also work like scoops, shoveling away snow to dig for food. They feed upon grasses, mushrooms, and other plants of the tundra. Male caribou grow large antlers and use them to battle for females. Female caribou grow smaller antlers and may use them to defend food from other females. As summer nears, caribou migrate north to feed, sometimes traveling more than 600 miles. When the first snows fall, they trek back south to more sheltered regions, completing a total migration of up to 1,600 miles.

CLIMATE CHANGE

The ice caps now are melting,
as seas begin to rise,
because of greenhouse gases
trapping heat inside our skies.
The polar bears and walruses
lose habitat each day,
as climate changes far too fast,
and sea ice breaks away.
Seals and penguins, arctic fox,
and birds are threatened too.
Finding a solution is
up to me and you!

The climate of our planet Earth is warming, largely because of human activity. Because we burn fossil fuels such as coal, oil, and natural gas for energy, our atmosphere is overloading with carbon dioxide. Carbon dioxide traps heat and pushes the temperature of our air higher, and melts lots of sea ice. The natural habitat of polar bears is on the sea ice of the Arctic, where they can hunt seals, their main source of food. But with sea ice now melting earlier in the spring, polar bears are forced onto land, where survival is more difficult. The reduction of sea ice in Antarctica may wipe out species of penguins living there. Pollution and oil spills can also kill wildlife and contaminate habitat. We can all do things to fight climate change. Ride a bike or walk instead of riding in a car. Recycle paper and plastics. Use energy-efficient light bulbs and products. Read how you can do more: https://www.nature.org/ourinitiatives/urgentissues/global-warming-climate-change/help/index.htm.

DOUGLAS FLORIAN is an acclaimed fine artist whose work has been described as having spontaneous immediacy and an ability to entice you to take a closer look at the everyday things we normally ignore.

At the age of six, Douglas participated in a collage workshop at the Museum of Modern Art, where he became fascinated by paper—colored, metallic, transparent, and textured. As an older child he encountered the work of such artists as Matisse, Picasso, and Magritte. He traces his love of words to the fifth grade, where he was introduced to Ogden Nash while browsing in a Queens library. "I love wordplay and dwell upon sounds of words as they roll off the tongue."

Douglas was educated at Queens College and the School of Visual Arts. A fortuitous encounter with a children's poetry anthology inspired him to write poems of his own. Douglas's poetry books often explore natural science and are illustrated in his distinctive style with media such as gouache, collage, or Cray-Pas on gesso-primed paper bags. His work encourages children to see and think and laugh.

BIBLIOGRAPHY

BOOKS

Kellett, Jenny. *The Ultimate Penguin Book for Kids: 100+ Amazing Penguin Facts, Photos, Quiz and BONUS Word Search Puzzle.* New York, Penguin Books for Kids, 2017.

Lopez, Barry. *Arctic Dreams*, New York, Vintage Books, 2014.

Rosing, Norbert. *The World of the Polar Bear*. Richmond Hill, Ontario, Canada, Firefly Books, 2010.

Taylor, Barbara. *Arctic & Antarctic*. New York, DK Eyewitness Books, 2012.

INTERNET

Smithsonian: The Arctic and the Antarctic
https://ocean.si.edu/ecosystems/poles/arctic-and-antarctic

National Oceanic and Atmospheric Administration, Pacific Marine Environmental Laboratory, Arctic Zone
https://www.pmel.noaa.gov/arctic-zone/animals.html

National Geographic, Meet the small Arctic animals that conquer their big polar world
https://video.nationalgeographic.com/video/animals-source/wild-life-with-bertie-gregory/0000016b-c3d4-df21-a37b-ffd627cb0000

47

IN MEMORY OF HENRI LALLOUZ—
A SWEET, SWEET FELLOW WHO LOVED THE BLUES

Library of Congress Cataloging-in-Publication Data

Names: Florian, Douglas, author, illustrator.
Title: ICE! : poems about polar life / Douglas Florian.
Description: First edition. | New York City : Holiday House, [2020]
Audience: Ages 7-10. | Audience: Grades 2-3. | Summary: "A kid-friendly
collection of more than twenty poems about the polar regions and the
animals that live there"—Provided by publisher.
Identifiers: LCCN 2019049806 | ISBN 9780823441013 (hardcover)
Subjects: LCSH: Animals—Polar regions—Juvenile poetry. | Animals—Polar
regions—Juvenile literature. | Children's poetry, American.
Polar regions—Juvenile poetry. | Polar regions—Juvenile literature.
Classification: LCC QL104 .F56 2020 | DDC 591.911—dc23
LC record available at https://lccn.loc.gov/2019049806
ISBN: 978-0-8234-4101-3 (hardcover)